Jungle
Jitters

Jungle
Jitters

Lisa Dalrymple

Orca *currents*

ORCA BOOK PUBLISHERS

Library and Archives Canada Cataloguing in Publication

Jungle jitters / Lisa Dalrymple.
(Orca currents)

Issued in print and electronic formats.
ISBN 978-1-4598-1349-6 (paperback).—ISBN 978-1-4598-1350-2 (pdf).—
ISBN 978-1-4598-1351-9 (epub)

I. Title. II. Series: Orca currents
PS8607.A47J86 2017   jC813'.6   C2016-904565-X
                          C2016-904566-8

First published in the United States, 2017
Library of Congress Control Number: 2016950082

Summary: In this high-interest novel for middle readers, Tate goes on a
school trip to the Amazon, where he must confront his worst fears.

*Orca Book Publishers is dedicated to preserving the environment and has
printed this book on Forest Stewardship Council® certified paper.*

Orca Book Publishers gratefully acknowledges the support for its
publishing programs provided by the following agencies: the Government
of Canada through the Canada Book Fund and the Canada Council
for the Arts,and the Province of British Columbia through
the BC Arts Council and the Book Publishing Tax Credit.

Cover photography by Getty Images
Author photo by Nadine Graham

ORCA BOOK PUBLISHERS
www.orcabook.com

Printed and bound in Canada.

20 19 18 17 • 4 3 2 1

For Marc, who has shared each adventure and every journey

Chapter One

Life was sweet—if I didn't think about becoming an anaconda's breakfast. I was sitting beside my best buddy, Dre, and we were flying along the Amazon River in a motorboat. Dre's attention was glued to the screen of his dad's old camera. He was all about getting video for his 912 YouTube fans. Noelle bounced along on the front seat, her black ponytail whipping about in the wind.

We were totally psyched to be on this trip. Mrs. Gallagher, our sixth-grade teacher, had been grinning since we got into the boat in Iquitos. Her husband had designed a school for a Yagua village, and because Dre, Noelle and I had done a lot of fundraising for the project, we all got to come to Peru with him while he inspected it.

In the back of the boat, Armando slowed the motor. "We are coming up to the *quebrada*, the creek, that will take us to the Jaguar Jungle Lodge."

His accent was cool, but I had to listen hard to understand what he said.

I turned back for one more look at the Amazon. I had pictured it snaking through overhanging vines and jungle growth, but it was miles wide—a super-size water highway.

Mr. Gallagher fidgeted with the brim of his Indiana Jones hat and gave me an impatient smile. Behind him, a flash of silver shot from the water. It streaked toward Armando's neck. He ducked, but he was too slow. The fish sank its teeth into his shoulder. I tried to call out, but my mouth was frozen.

That wasn't the case for Armando.

"Guys! Guys!" he shouted. "Look at this!"

He gestured to the long silver creature attached to him. Okay, the fish wasn't physically attached to his body. But it had latched onto his T-shirt with fangs the size of my baby fingers—and that was pretty much the same thing.

His shirt ripped as Armando tore the fish off him.

"Freshwater barracuda," he explained. "They get excited by the moving boat. They think we are something to eat."

He snorted and tossed it overboard. I edged away from the side of the boat while Noelle laughed nervously and put her hand on my arm. She did that sometimes in math class too, but I knew she was only trying to see past me out the window. Dre pointed his camera at the water where the barracuda had disappeared. Wasn't anybody worried that a *vampire fish* had jumped out of the river and sunk its teeth into one of us?

Dre was probably just ticked that we didn't get a photo. I dug my phone out of my backpack and hit the Home button. Zero bars. But I didn't need reception to take pictures.

We rounded a bend in the quebrada. Murky water *lap-lapped* against the sides of our boat, and vines trailed from overhanging treetops. *This* was the Amazon I had imagined. Bugs droned around us, and sweat plastered my

jaguar-spotted life jacket to my back.
Armando had said a quebrada was a
creek, but I didn't think I'd even be able
to touch the bottom. *Not* that I planned
to find out.

A couple of boys were paddling a
hollowed-out tree trunk. I shuddered
at the thought of being that close to
the dark, muddy water. If I fell in,
I wouldn't even be able to see my own
feet. Never mind what was swimming
just below them.

I wondered if they thought we
looked funny in our life jackets and
sunhats while they glided along in their
faded shirts and shorts, looking totally
comfortable with the river. They stared
at us as we passed. I guessed they hadn't
seen that many people with dark skin
and dreadlocks like Dre's. He held his
camera to one side and waved. "Hey,
Tate, you should wave too," he said,
elbowing me in the ribs.

"Tate?" Mr. Gallagher asked his wife. "I thought you said his name was Ethan."

"It is. Tate's short for Potato, I believe."

Mr. Gallagher nodded as if to say, *That makes total sense*, while his expression said, *That makes no sense at all*. Mrs. G. looked apologetic. I knew she would never tell him the joke, so I explained. "Like a boring old potato."

Noelle punched me on the shoulder. "Oh, come on! You know it's not because you're boring."

"Oh, really?"

"No. It was that speech you did in third grade. It was…um…impressive. Who knew anyone could talk for a full twelve minutes about potatoes?"

"See what I mean?" I said. "Boring."

But over the next five days, I was determined to take on anything the Amazon could throw at me. No one would ever call me boring again. That is, if I survived.

Chapter Two

We docked at the Jaguar Jungle Lodge, and Armando made sure we left our life jackets under our seats. "If you go out in the fishing boat, you will need to bring a life jacket from the lodge. These ones stay here for my passengers. If my boat flips, at least nobody will drown."

Ha! I knew what would happen if I fell in wearing one of those life jackets.

I'd be a yummy chunk of bait dangling from a jaguar-spotted lure, enticing anything lurking below. I gave Armando a sarcastic smile. "Well, that's good to know."

He beamed.

We hauled our backpacks onto the dock along with the three boxes of books we'd brought. Once we were on the riverbank, Armando pointed at a wooden shed.

"Go inside and get some rubber boots," he said. "It is always swampy here. Also, they will protect your feet."

"Protect our feet from what?" Dre whispered to me.

Did it matter? I gulped.

Still, I was more comfortable on land. At least I'd be able to see what was coming for me—and I could run.

I found a pair of size 10s and clomped along behind Dre and his camera. Two men with machetes slashed at the under-growth, clearing paths around the lodge.

8

Turning the camera toward his face, Dre whispered to his viewers, "You can already feel the jungle creeping back again. Mwah-ha-ha!"

A couple of kids watched us arrive. They had copper-toned skin and black hair like the boys in the canoe, but I could tell they weren't from around here. The girl's hoodie gave them away. It looked like something you could buy at the mall. "Maria and Oscar!" Armando called to them as he walked past. "Can you take these guys to the canteen? We will meet you there after we register."

Maria grinned at us. Oscar was too busy poking a spider with a stick.

"What's he doing?" Dre asked.

"Oh, just trying to get attention," Maria said.

Noelle laughed. "Yeah. My little brother is like that too."

"This place is driving me crazy." Maria groaned. "I have no one to talk to except *him*. Half the staff only speaks Yagua. And Mom works all the time."

Oscar coaxed the spider onto his hand.

"So you're not guests here?" Dre asked.

Maria shook her head. "Oh, we haven't been guests for months. Mom worked it out so she can do housekeeping until she *finds herself* or whatever."

Noelle screamed. Maria jumped.

Oscar dangled the spider between two fingers. In his other hand, a detached spider leg still wriggled.

"Seriously, Oscar?" Maria reached out to swat him.

He dropped the spider, which scurried into a hole in the ground.

"Come on." Maria sighed. "Let's get some supper."

We followed her up the steps to a wooden walkway. It was sheltered by the low-hanging roof of the canteen. Inside, gas lanterns flickered on the tables. Although it was only late afternoon, already the last of the daylight couldn't make it through the heavy canopy of trees, and there was no electricity in this part of the jungle.

"This is like summer camp," Noelle said.

"N'uh-uh," Oscar said. "The snakes here are *way* bigger."

Noelle shot him the look she usually saved for her own little brother.

Maria showed us to the buffet table. I had been excited about trying the fish, but they still had their heads on, and that creeped me out. Instead, I helped myself to two different kinds of potatoes. Not super adventurous. I was looking around for something different when Maria said the plantains were pretty good. They looked like giant grilled bananas. I put one on my plate and followed the others to a table. Two lanterns made it just bright enough to see.

"This is perfect for campfire stories," I said.

Dre rubbed his hands together and grinned. "People say our summer camp is built on the site of an old dueling ground. A couple hundred years ago, this guy Horace challenged his brother to a fight. They dueled until Horace got his head sliced off. His arms and legs kept thrashing as his body fell to the ground, and his foot booted his own head into the lake. Now every full moon, the ghost of Headless Horace flies through the camp, slashing his sword around and hoping to find a new head."

Maria snorted. "Oh, there are legends in the Amazon that are *way* creepier than that!" Her face grew serious as she leaned across the table. "Have you ever heard of El Tunchi?"

As she said his name, the lamp at the other end of our table sputtered out. The girls looked at each other and giggled.

"Go on," Noelle said.

Maria lowered her voice. "They say El Tunchi is the spirit of those who took their last breath in the jungle. A long time ago, a man brought his son and daughter to steal all the jungle's healing plants and sell them in the city. One night, when the father was away, an old tribal woman warned the kids, *Your father is a selfish man. He won't listen to the elders, but El Tunchi will take care of the jungle, even if it means taking care of him.*

"She told them that El Tunchi moves through the rainforest, whistling *fui fui fui fui fui*. The only way to protect yourself is to pretend you don't hear. Don't even mention the noises. And don't hurt the plants or animals! If El Tunchi thinks you mean harm, he won't leave you alone. The *fui fui fui* will grow louder, until it drives you insane. And *then* he will get you!"

Dre jumped and shouted. Noelle laughed.

"No, seriously," he said. "Something brushed against my legs."

Noelle's eyes widened. "I feel it too! There's something under the table."

Maria growled and pushed back her chair. "Oscar…"

Her brother crawled out beside her. He hid his grin behind the palm leaf in his hand. Maria grabbed it and brushed him away.

She turned back into the lamplight and continued her story. "So the next day, the girl didn't want to work, but there was no way she was staying home alone. She went into the jungle with her brother, and again he started ripping out every herb he could find. All of a sudden, he stopped and said, *Do you hear that?*

"The girl shivered. But she said, *No, I hear nothing.*

"*How can you not hear it?* her brother asked.

"*Even if I did, I would just ignore it and leave,* she said.

"Her brother snorted. *You seriously believe that crazy old lady?*

"He kept working. He started humming to drown out the sound. Then he started singing and shouting. Anything to block out the whistle. By the time his sister took him home, he had covered his ears and was screaming. The people of the village knew El Tunchi was near.

"The girl tried to put him in bed, but he just stood by the window, whistling loudly. *Fui fui fui fui fui.* In the end, she left him in his room and sat with her back against his door all night. He whistled for hours and hours—until suddenly he stopped.

"The girl heard him whimpering, and a chill seeped out from under his door. She started shivering again.

"Next thing, she heard her brother screaming! Cries of terror like she'd never heard before. The room was being ripped apart. The girl tried to move, but she was frozen. She heard something being dragged away, and her brother's screams grew quieter. She hauled herself up and threw open the door, but there was no sign of the boy.

"He was never seen alive again."

For a moment, there were only the sounds of the night creatures in the jungle. Noelle twisted her hair around a finger, and Dre cleared his throat. They didn't seem scared. Were they both just better than me at hiding the fact that they were totally freaking out?

Personally, I was almost peeing my pants. Now, on top of worrying about vampire fish and everything else that wanted to take a bite out of this Potato, I was panicked about harming the rainforest.

Chapter Three

Supper was finished when we left the canteen and followed the raised walkway to the guest lodge. The jungle was even louder than it had been in the day. Unseen creatures croaked and shrieked in the darkness.

Maria pointed to the right. "Dre and Tate, your room is around there. Noelle, you're out in the staff building with us.

You have the room beside your teacher. Oscar and I are on the other side."

It took a moment for it to sink in to Noelle that she would be on her own.

"How come everyone else gets a roommate?" she asked quietly.

Maria shrugged. "Maybe I can sleep over some nights. That would be so awesome! It would get me away from Oscar for a while."

Oscar folded his arms and *humph*ed, but Noelle's face brightened. Even so, I thought she still looked unsure. As they headed down to the lawn, Maria turned back.

"Don't forget to leave your muddy boots outside your room, guys!" she called.

At our door, I fumbled with the key while Dre dug out his flashlight and camera. Once inside, he started recording again.

"Whoa!" he said, taking in the mesh that lined the outer walls and the ceiling.

"They really take their bug protection seriously around here."

Through the screen above us, I noticed the sloped underside of the lodge roof. "And there are two beds, of course. One for me and one for my roommate," he told his viewers as he swept the camera toward me. "You all remember my redheaded buddy, Taterman, here."

His flashlight blinded me as I squinted into the camera. I had appeared in many of his past videos, not always by choice.

"And check out the mosquito nets around the beds!" Dre said, untying one and letting it hang loose on its frame.

I opened my pack and found the pajamas Mom had bought me. They were under the mountain of new underwear she had packed. You'd think I was here for a month. Dre was still examining the mosquito nets.

While he was distracted, I stepped out of my pants to change.

"So you tuck the net under the mattress all around you, and it keeps you completely safe," Dre told his viewers. "Well, at least from the bugs. Right, Tater?"

He spun around and pointed his camera at me. There I was, in brand-new briefs so white they practically glowed in the dark.

Dre almost choked on his laughter as he announced, "There's the Tatester now in his old-school *tighty-whities*!"

He snorted and turned off the camera.

My face was burning, but getting embarrassed would be a lame-o Potato thing to do, so I tried to shrug it off. "You know my mom."

"*Shyeah*! At least Granny lets me pick out my own boxers."

Dre's parents had died in a car accident before I moved to Rockton Heights.

Sometimes I'd forget and complain about my mom or dad. I felt like a total jerk every time. I fumbled with the mosquito netting on my bed. By the time I was safely tucked in, Dre was grinning at me from inside his sleeping bag.

"Good night, sleep tight, don't let the jaguars bite!"

"Heh-heh. Good one," I said and clicked off my flashlight.

It was easier to laugh when the lights were on. But now, in the dark, every noise in the jungle was amplified. How did anyone sleep with all those tree frogs singing?

And…was that a snuffling noise?

Fshhle…fshhle…

It sounded like it was outside our door.

Fshhle…fshhle…fshhle…

Or was it really *fui fui fui*?

Oh, that's stupid, I told myself. I'm sure it's just…what? An Amazonian raccoon?

Now it was scrambling up the wall. Was it headed for the screen above our heads? Was it looking for a way in? For the first time since we'd started this trip, I missed Mom. And Dad. He was the one who usually came when I had a nightmare.

Dre rolled over in the dark. He groaned. "Awwwww, snap!"

"What?"

"I gotta pee."

My jaw dropped. "You're going out there? The bathroom's all the way around the other side of the lodge."

Surely he could hear the noise. What did it mean if I was the only one who could hear it? After Maria's story, I was keeping my mouth shut.

Dre grunted. "I got no choice."

The beam of his flashlight bounced around as he wriggled out of his sleeping bag.

Was he crazy? Nothing would get me out from under my mosquito netting—not that its flimsy mesh was any protection against the wild animal prowling above my face.

Dre cracked open the door. And then he was gone.

I realized I didn't hear him lock it. Dre never locked doors, not even to his school locker. I was alone in an unlocked room in the middle of the jungle, and something outside was desperate to get in.

I listened, trying to figure out where it might be. The peeps and croaks drowned out all other noises. Maybe Dre had scared the creature off. Or had the creature carried Dre off instead?

Chapter Four

I listened for what seemed like an hour, but the noises didn't come back before I fell asleep. And neither did my buddy.

When I woke in the morning, Dre was tying his laces at the end of his bed. Had the night creature been a figment of my imagination? As I rolled over, he grabbed his camera and was halfway out of the room before he realized I was awake.

"I gotta go meet Mrs. G. in the canteen," he said without turning around.

Before I could ask why, he darted out onto the walkway, pulling the door closed behind him.

What was that about? He was acting different, not Dre-ish. The night before, he had been brave enough to run out into the dark jungle. But today he was nervous about even looking me in the eye. Had something happened, or was I imagining this too?

With the room to myself, I got dressed, new tighty-whities and all. I shoved my feet into my old sneakers and then ran toward the sounds of breakfast.

Mrs. G. looked up as the canteen door creaked shut behind me. "How'd you sleep, Ethan?"

I attempted to look refreshed. "Great!"

I could see she didn't believe me. But she wouldn't rat me out. Mrs. G.

always said we redheads had to stick together.

Still, Noelle could tell I was lying. "Seriously?"

Before she could say more, a woman approached our table with a tray of porridge. There was a picture of a boy band on her shirt, and she had thick black hair like Maria's.

"Hey, you guys," Maria said. "This is my mom, Isabelle."

Isabelle looked at me. "So I hear you and Dre had monkeys last night? Sometimes they go *loco*—crazy—on the roof of that guest lodge!"

"Oh, I thought I heard something," I said, trying to sound unconcerned. "I'm so used to raccoons and bears and stuff—when we're camping."

"Bears?" Maria's eyebrows shot up.

"Yeah." I changed the subject quickly. "I can't wait to see the school today."

"Neither can Mr. G.!" Mrs. Gallagher said. "He says he and I should go on ahead with the guides."

Isabelle nodded. "Armando and Sebedo want to go early to make sure the path is clear. But if you're going with them, you've got to get moving."

She picked up one of Mrs. Gallagher's bags and carried it outside. Dre arrived at the table with two cups of cocoa and a plate of pineapple for us to share. Maybe I had only imagined his weirdness in the room.

"So we'll meet you kids at the swamp," Mrs. G. called back from the door.

My mouth was full of pineapple.

"Fwamp? Wha fwamp?" I asked Maria.

She laughed. "You'll have to canoe across it to get to the Yagua village."

Canoe across a weedy swamp in the heart of the Amazon jungle? I almost choked.

"I'll show you guys the way after we get your stuff from the rooms."

Oscar grabbed his sister's arm. "Can I come?"

"Not this morning," Maria said. "You stay with Mom. She might need your help."

Oscar followed us as we left the canteen. On the grass below the walkway, there was a flash of yellow and blue as a toucan lifted its bill.

"Señor Diego!" Oscar shouted. He pushed past me and jumped down the steps. The bird fluttered a few feet away. Oscar chased after it.

Turning back, he sang out, "Remember to shake out your boots before you put them on. You don't want to squish any tarantulas!"

Chapter Five

"Tarantulas?" I asked Maria.

"Oh, just ignore him," she said, turning so that Oscar could hear her shout, "It only happened *the one time*!"

I didn't need to hear anymore. I hustled back to our room with Dre. I found one of my boots and hunted around for the other. Dre shook his until he was positive they were empty. He put them on and stood watching me. Wrapping his dreads in his purple tie-dyed bandanna, he was ready to take on the jungle! I was still searching.

"Where did you leave it?" he asked.

"Right here," I said. "Obviously."

"Maybe someone took it," he suggested. "Hey, maybe it was the monkeys!"

I gave him a look. "What would a monkey do with a size 10 rubber boot?"

"Maybe you stepped in fruit or something. I dunno."

I didn't know either. The only thing I did know was that my stomach felt hollow at the thought of being left behind because I didn't have boots.

"This totally sucks," I said.

"Hey!" said Dre. "I'll bet I could get you another one. There were tons in that shed."

I started to tell him how awesome he was, but he was already thundering off toward the quebrada. He was back before I'd zipped up my daypack.

We met Maria and Noelle in the garden behind the kitchen. Clusters of bananas and papayas grew all around, and who knew pineapples don't grow on trees? They grow on the ground, like cabbage, only surrounded by spiky leaves—which looked like better protection from the animals than a mesh ceiling and walls.

Dre knelt down beside the fruit and held his camera at arm's length.

"So, here I am with a wild pineapple," he began.

Maria pointed to two parrots, one red and one blue, preening on a branch in front of us.

"Hey, Dre, get a shot of those guys," she said. "They think they're our pets."

Noelle approached the birds, rubbing her fingers together as if she had a nut for them.

"I wouldn't get too close," Maria warned.

"Why not?"

"They're really bratty," she explained. "And they bite."

Noelle pulled her hand back. She waved it at the jungle around us.

"What doesn't?" she asked.

I grinned. Cute *and* sarcastic!

"Well, Señor Diego's okay. He likes Oscar and me because we feed him. Everyone else just blames him when something goes wrong around here."

Dre looked away from his camera.

"Like what?" he asked. "Does he take stuff?"

"All the time," Maria answered. "How'd you know?"

"Lucky guess," Dre said, but he winked at me.

Dre wasn't taking this seriously if he thought a toucan could make off with a boot.

We followed Maria down a path into the jungle. With each step, mud sucked at my feet, pulling me off-balance. Ahead, Maria shuffled across a log. I followed, but my boots were so caked with mud that they had no grip. Size 10 suddenly felt huge. I had no idea how deep the swamp was. If I slipped off the log, what would be waiting for me in there?

Noelle called to Maria, "Are there many dangerous animals around here?"

It was good to hear her ask the question that had been preying on me since we'd arrived.

"Like jaguars?" Maria asked.

I looked back to see Noelle's face turn white.

"No," Maria said. "No jaguars near here."

Something in the way she said *jaguars* made me question what *was* out there. I didn't ask.

Maria pointed at a tree in front of us. It stretched up until it disappeared into the jungle's canopy above, its trunk so big that it had folded in on itself. Some of its creases had caverns I could stand inside.

"This is a ceiba tree," Maria said.

Noelle ventured closer and waved me in. "Come see."

I peered into one of the creases and saw a movement. Something was alive in there. But what? As I leaned in, a bat shuddered and opened its wings. I swear its beady eyes were staring at me. Weren't they blind?

The bat's movement set off a ripple effect. Hundreds of wings folded and refolded. Maybe I should get out of there before they swarmed. Plus, bat poo stank worse than my hamster cage at home.

But standing in a cavern full of bats in the Amazon was definitely not a boring thing to do. Dre should get a picture of me to show the kids back at school.

"Hey, Dre!"

I turned around and found his camera was already in my face. Now Dre was shooting an extreme close-up of my right nostril. Once again, his video would capture me at my best!

I pulled away from the lens and cleared my throat. "Maria, what kind of bats are these?"

"Fruit bats," she said.

"So they don't drink blood?"

"No."

She paused and then smirked. "Not these ones."

Not concerned about the camera anymore, I whispered to Dre, "Why does everything around here have to be so bitey or stingy?"

"Or stabby," he said.

He pointed the camera off to our right. The path led down a steep bank. Fortunately, there was a tree to grab on to right in the middle of the path. Not so fortunately, its trunk looked like my nana's pincushion—if all of the needles had their sharp ends pointing out.

"Yeah. Watch out for that," Maria said before she turned away to point something out to Noelle. But I was already looking past the stabby tree. At the bottom of the bank, something moved. I heard the cries of a frightened animal, and a creature staggered out of the jungle.

It was Oscar—but he was covered with bugs. With pleading eyes, he reached out to me.

Chapter Six

Oscar's arms and neck were a moving carpet of bugs. I shuddered. Talk about your skin crawling!

His eyes were round and wild. "Help me, Tate!"

He swatted at his flesh, lurching and jerking like a zombie, squashing the bugs until his skin was covered in smeared guts. He must be losing his mind.

Dre's camera whirred as he zoomed in.

"Quit it, Dre!" I snapped. "We need to help him, not film him!"

At that moment, I knew I was going to be *un*lame, and for once Dre was going to get it on video.

I stepped forward with my right foot, but I paused. Did I really want to run toward a crazy kid covered in who-knew-what-kind-of-flesh-eating Amazon insects? What good was a video if I didn't survive?

My moment's hesitation was long enough for my right foot to begin sliding forward. As I scrambled, trying to dig my heel into the dirt, my toes caught under a root, and I toppled forward. The world turned into a bumpy blur of over, under, over, under. At any moment, I would be impaled on the pincushion tree.

Except I wasn't.

It was far from the prettiest of landings, but I stopped without crashing. Lying at Oscar's feet, I looked up. He laughed and pointed at me with his bug-gut-covered hand.

"What's so funny?" I choked out. "I'm here to rescue you."

"From what? These?" He crushed up more of the insects. "They're just smushed termites! Works better than your bug spray."

He ran back toward the lodge. I sprawled on the dirt, watching him go. Terrific! Even the eight-year-old knew I was a total noob.

I called after him, "I'll smush you, you little dweeb!" Oh great! Now I sounded like our grumpy old neighbor who shook his fist every time we walked on his grass. Oscar looked back, his bottom lip trembling. I *almost* felt bad. Then he sneered and stuck out his tongue. My guilty feeling passed.

Noelle gasped as she and Maria arrived at the top of the bank.

Beside them, Dre zoomed in on me. "And here you will see, my buddy Tater displaying his usual issue with gravity."

He waved down at me. "Way to go there, Gravi-Tater!"

I gave him a halfhearted thumbs-up. The Amazon was definitely giving me opportunities to prove I wasn't boring. I was becoming the Potato with pizzazz, but for all the wrong reasons.

Noelle found her way down to where I was pulling myself to my feet. She picked up my pack, wiped off some mud and passed it to me.

"Are you okay?"

I was pretty sure she wasn't asking about my pride. "Yeah, I'm just dandy."

Dre whooped. "Oh, I am *so* gonna hit one thousand subscribers when I get this baby uploaded!"

"Hey!" Maria said. "Do you think video of a baby sloth would help your numbers? I could take you to see one if we get Armando to clear the back path tomorrow."

I didn't know who looked more thrilled. Dre at Maria's suggestion? Or Maria at seeing she'd made Dre smile? Watching them grin at each other was nauseating.

"Oh, cut it, you two!" I groaned.

"Yeah." Noelle offered me a high five. "Before we regurgi-Tate."

I slapped her hand, and we heard Armando shout through the trees, "Guys! Guys! We're over here."

He and Sebedo were waiting with Mr. and Mrs. G. at a watery spot in the swamp. Two canoes bobbed in a field of aquatic weeds. They were so thick that I couldn't tell where the land ended and the water began.

Maria pointed to a lily pad covered in toothlike spikes. It had to be bigger than a queen-size bed!

"Huge, right?" she said. "Everything's bigger here. Last month Sebedo found a five-meter-long anaconda."

"In here?" I asked.

Somehow I knew her answer even before I saw her nod.

"That's too cool!" Dre said.

Part of me agreed with him. But another part, the Potato part, wanted to point out that we were getting ready to cross that same swamp in two rickety canoes.

Mr. Gallagher was already sitting in Sebedo's canoe, drumming his fingers on the seat in front of him. Noelle got the hint and climbed in. She waved goodbye to Maria, who had to go back to the lodge and look after Oscar. Sebedo pushed off from the shore.

Dre and I settled in the middle of Armando's canoe, a pool of sludgy water at our feet.

As Mrs. G. climbed in the back, she put her hand on Dre's shoulder. "How are you feeling?"

"Awesome." Dre handed her the long stick Armando passed back.

Peruvian canoes did not come with paddles. Instead, Armando and Mrs. G. used the poles to push us through the swamp. Our boat sat heavy in the water.

Armando frowned. "We might get stuck. It is quite shallow here when it is not the rainy season."

Seeing that Dre was recording again, I pulled myself up taller. "Can I do anything to help?"

"Yes, that is your job," Armando said. "When we get stuck on a log, you and Dre rock from side to side.

Mrs. Gallagher and I will try to push the boat over it."

"But we could tip," I said.

"We will try not to." Armando chuckled.

Dre pointed his camera at me as I swallowed the rest of my questions. I was sure I wouldn't like Armando's answers anyway.

As we moved through the weeds, Mrs. Gallagher gushed about the scenery, but I didn't see it. I was on the lookout for anacondas or piranhas or... *were there crocodiles*?

Ahead of me, Armando pulled his pole out of the water and rested it across his knees. Turning back, he held a finger to his lips.

"Shhhh. Do you hear that?"

Hear what?

I couldn't hear anything. As I turned to look at Dre, my rubber boots squeaked.

Armando's eyes opened wide. I froze. I didn't dare breathe. Had our guide heard a ferocious jungle creature? Or was he scared that something had heard us?

Chapter Seven

Then I heard it. Grunts and groans. They were getting closer.

"Dinosaur bird," Armando whispered.

He pointed to our right. "In the trees."

What the heck was a dinosaur bird?

More noises. Squawking and wheezing on our left.

"Another one!" Armando said.

I gripped my seat. "They're everywhere."

And yet Armando pushed us deeper into the heart of dinosaur territory. Vines grasped at the sides of our boat. Grasses and shrubs leaned in toward us.

Through the leaves, I caught a flash of blue. Then another. Beaked faces peered out at us. Heads bobbed. Wings flapped in protest. But the birds kept their distance. They were angry, but they didn't look like dinosaurs—more like punk pheasants with scraggly mohawks, blue faces and piercing red eyes. They reminded me of Dad's costume for the retro dance last year.

"They are hoatzins," Armando said. "They have been on Earth for millions of years. The babies have claws on their wings like some of the dinosaurs did."

We trespassed farther into their territory. Soon it was not the birds we heard but the rhythm of drums. Armando steered our canoe in to join Noelle and Mr. Gallagher, who were waiting on the shore. Sebedo had gone ahead to prepare his village for our arrival.

The air pulsed with the energy of drums and flutes. We climbed a hill and arrived in a cluster of thatched huts. Red-painted faces turned toward us, and the women wore red cotton skirts. The men wore skirts too, but theirs were made of palm leaves. I didn't know where to look without staring. For a second, my eyes met a boy's. He was smiling. Realizing that people were happy to see us, I took a deep breath and walked into the village.

The ground sloped toward a river, and a tour-company boat approached the shore. The Yagua women danced as visitors from America or Europe clambered onto the bank. Yagua children took the tourists' hands and pulled them to a shelter to buy crafts.

They were about to approach us too until Sebedo ran out of the large circular hut in the middle of the village, waving his arms as though we were cousins he hadn't seen in years. He spoke to Armando in Yagua and guided us over to a new building on stilts. It was the school!

Dre panned up with his camera. The floor was level with our heads, and the room along the front looked more like a screened-in porch at a summer cottage than a classroom.

Inside, Dre turned the camera on me and joked, "You feel that nice breeze off the river?"

I twisted my face. It was hot and sticky—inside the school and out—and I was sure my hair was plastered rather unflatteringly to my head.

Mr. Gallagher took off his hat, extended his arms and announced, "Well, this is it, folks!"

He spoke so that the microphone on Dre's camera could pick up everything he said. "In the back are rooms for the teacher and bathrooms with composting toilets."

Sebedo beamed and said something to Armando.

"He wants me to show you the best part," Armando translated.

We followed him through a doorway into a room lined with bookshelves and protected by solid wooden walls.

"This," said Armando, "will be a library for the village!"

Mr. Gallagher looked so proud he might burst. "The books will be kept dry even when the river floods."

I looked at Noelle and knew exactly what she was thinking—we hadn't brought enough books. I swear I saw her mind kick into warp speed.

"We should run a book drive at school!" she said.

There was no holding her back now. Dre and I knew from experience. No doubt she was already counting on us to help her give a presentation to all of Rockton Heights.

Noelle pointed to the door. "Dre, get out there and get lots of video of the village children. Tate, you use your phone to get still photos for a slideshow."

Dre rolled his eyes, but he grinned at me as our group left the school.

It wasn't hard to find the children. They were waiting for us. A young girl took Noelle's hand. I snapped a picture, thinking Noelle would like that. A group of kids tugged Dre over to the market. I snapped another.

Under the shelter, women dressed in grass chest plates displayed jewelry made of shells and teeth. Noelle crouched down and dug in her bag for some coins while her new friend tied a string of seeds around her neck.

A Yagua man directed Dre to a mat filled with wooden carvings and weapons. Dre's eyes gleamed as he picked up a blowgun.

"Yagua hunters use these to shoot poison darts," Armando said.

Dre grinned. "*Sick*!"

Mrs. Gallagher smiled, took the blowgun from him and put it back on the mat. My older brother, Noah, would love a blowgun, but I figured Mom's reaction would be the same as Mrs. G.'s. Instead, I bought him a red tribal mask decorated with teeth.

I took pictures of kids with drums or playing with dolls. By the time we left the village, the battery on my phone was almost dead.

That night in the canteen, Noelle scrolled through my pictures. "Hey, these are great, Tate!"

Maria shook her head. "I'm sorry, but I need to ask. Is Tate a nickname?"

I sighed. "It's short for Potato."

She raised her eyebrows.

"Because I'm boring," I said.

"Potatoes aren't boring," Maria said. "There are *thousands* of different kinds of them in Peru. And if you don't cook them properly, you know you can die?"

"No surprise there." I laughed. "Even the potatoes around here can kill you."

Noelle glanced up. "I think your phone just ran out of juice, Tate."

"Don't worry," Maria said, reaching over to look at it. "You can leave it on that table with your adapter. Armando charges our stuff overnight. There's a generator in his village."

"I better charge my camera too," Dre said, taking off his bandanna and wiping his forehead. "But first, how about some entertainment?"

He set the camera on the table and turned it so Noelle and Maria could see.

The canteen came alive with the noises of the jungle, followed by Oscar groaning. "Help me, Tate!"

Maria choked back a laugh as she watched her brother covered in termites and me flopping down the hill. Noelle glanced over at me. I couldn't tell what she was thinking. But it seemed they were all getting a kick out of my performance.

"I'll just pop back and get my phone charger." I stood up. I understood that Dre wanted to look like a funny guy in front of Maria, but why did he have to do it by featuring *my* awkward acrobatics?

Chapter Eight

I knew from life with an older brother
that if anyone realized I was upset about
the video, I'd only get teased worse.
I took my time walking back to the
canteen, and as I returned to my seat,
I noticed that Oscar had joined our
table. But story time was over. That
was good. I was getting tired of Dre's
videos making me look like a loser.

I felt awkward around the others now, but at least nobody noticed.

That night, as everyone else slept, I heard the roar of rain approaching through the jungle. It rushed in over the trees and raced toward our building. Raindrops pelted the roof. I pulled my sleeping bag up and rolled over to face the wall, imagining I was in a blanket fort at the cottage.

As the rain slowed, I heard another noise. An animal on the roof again? But tonight it sounded closer, like it was already in the room. And I might have heard the door *snick* shut.

Had Dre gone out to the bathroom? I flicked on my flashlight. His dreadlocks were sticking out the top of his sleeping bag. If he was here, what I had heard? The monkeys? Señor Diego? El Tunchi?

I swept the flashlight beam around the room, telling myself that I was not scared of a ghost story. No way. This Tate was not a lame, boring potato. This Tate was a Peruvian potato. The Tate-nator. Wild, poisonous and strong enough to take on the Amazon!

Still, I was happy when the rain got louder again. I pulled my sleeping bag over my head to keep out the jungle's dampness. At least, that's what I told myself it was for.

We woke to sunlight filtering through our window and the *drip, drip* of water off the trees outside. I found my boots on the sheltered walkway to the left of our room.

"At least they're where they're supposed to be today," I said to Dre.

He nodded, picking his up from the right-hand side of the door. But I remembered him leaving them beside mine. Maybe he had been out in the night after all.

"We can't wear these in the canteen," Dre said. "They're nasty!"

I held out my muddy daypack. "I don't think Mrs. G. would want this at breakfast either."

We wore our runners and left our dirty things outside when we went in to eat. Dre found his camera charged and waiting for him on the table, but my phone wasn't there. I asked Noelle and Mrs. Gallagher if they had seen it.

Mrs. G.'s brow wrinkled. "It was there earlier when I stopped in for coffee."

"Señor Diego again?" Dre winked at Maria.

"Could be." She smiled.

She must have noticed my glance at the door. I was sure a toucan couldn't open it. I thought about our own door *snick*ing closed in the night.

"Sometimes he sneaks in behind people," Maria explained.

Mrs. G. seemed to find that funny.

"Let me ask Armando about your phone," she said. "I need to find him to tell him I'm not coming today."

She gave Dre a funny look. Nobody else noticed. Was something weird going on with him?

By the time we had finished breakfast, Mrs. G. hadn't come back.

"Can we wait a little longer, guys?" I asked.

Maria shook her head. "Not if you want to take the other path and see the sloths today."

"Oh yeah, we do!" Dre said, digging through his bag. He pulled out a rainbow-colored bandanna I'd never seen before and wrapped it around his dreads.

"Yeah, but *I* can't take pictures if I don't have my phone." I knew I sounded whiny, so I laughed. "Please don't make me irri-Tated."

Maria giggled. "I'm sure Dre will take enough pictures for all of us."

Almost immediately, Dre's camera was in her face as he snapped a photo. "Dre!" she gasped. "Delete that!"

"Maybe later." He grinned.

"We can't wait any longer," she said, "or my brother'll get here, and we'll have to bring him."

Oscar walked into the canteen just in time to hear her. He stuck out his tongue, and Dre snapped another picture. This time Maria laughed. Her brother scowled. As we walked past him to the door, I wanted to tell Oscar I knew how he felt.

We changed into our muddy boots and followed Maria to the back path. The ground was boggy, and there were a zillion bugs. It sounded like the jungle was full of chainsaws, not insects.

"Hang on a sec, guys," I said. "I think I need more bug spray."

I swung my daypack around to my chest and fumbled with the zipper. Inside, my hand touched something hard and unfamiliar. I dug about, but there was another thing firm and cool to the touch...and something else. I froze. Were things moving in there?

I yanked my hand back and lifted the flap. Inside my bag was a squirming nest of sausage-sized centipedes. Some had curled into balls, and others were crawling through my stuff.

"Gross!" I dropped the pack, and bugs flew everywhere.

"Ew," Maria said as she bent down and plucked my repellant out of the wriggling mess. Holding it out to me, she laughed. "But they're not going to bite you or anything."

I swear I wanted to abandon my stuff right there. But if Maria could stick her hand into the writhing pile of bugs, I guessed I had to suck it up too.

I grabbed one strap of my daypack. Holding the whole thing away from my body, I shook it out. My sunscreen and Swiss Army knife fell to the ground, and bugs rained down around them.

"Why would they be in there anyway?" Noelle asked. "Did you have food or something?"

"No," I said. "Plus, the zipper was closed. How would they even get in?"

"Someone might have put them there," Maria said.

Dre grinned. "Maybe you ticked off the evil toucan again."

I couldn't believe he would joke about this.

"Yeah." Maria laughed. "Believe me. You do not wanna mess with that bird!"

I held up my bag. Who knew what was still in there? I didn't want to carry it anymore.

"Are you taking it back to the lodge?" Noelle asked.

Maria groaned. "We gotta get moving or we'll be late."

Dre turned toward the path.

"You in, or are you out?" he asked.

"I'm coming." I sighed and slung my bag on my back.

Dre and Maria walked ahead. I was glad. It made it easier not to talk to them. I hung back with Noelle. She seemed to get that I wasn't in a super-chatty mood. Not like Dre.

"So how'd you end up living in the middle of the jungle?" he asked Maria.

"Beats the heck out of me." She snorted. "After Dad bailed, Mom decided we were taking off to find her roots or something. Her grandparents were from Iquitos, like, a zillion years ago. But it's rough, you know? I miss my friends."

"Girlfriends?" Dre asked.

Maria turned to grin at him, and I saw her face flush.

"Yeah. No boyfriend." She hip-checked him to the edge of the path before she continued. "And I think Oscar really misses Dad."

Dre nodded. "That can be tough on a kid."

He launched into his story about growing up without a father.

"There!" Maria stopped and pointed above our heads.

High in the trees, a baby sloth clung to its mother, her gangly arms and legs wrapped around a trunk. I heard the whir of the camera. Dre zoomed in close.

But I was focused on my own thoughts. I couldn't believe Dre had been ready to trek out here without me instead of waiting for me to drop off my bag. And I didn't believe a toucan had stolen my stuff either. What I thought was that somehow, since we'd arrived in this jungle, I'd done something to upset someone. But who? Or what?

Chapter Nine

We met the guides and Mr. G. at the canoes. Unlike the day before, we didn't get any surprises on our way to the Yagua village—only after we arrived. There were no drums, no painted faces and no men in leafy skirts. Without any tours to entertain, today the villagers were looking at *us*.

I had figured Dre's dark skin would get a lot of attention, but it was my paleness that stood out. Even the grown-ups were watching me. Noelle's friend from the day before ran over to take my hand, but I was sure she just wanted a closer look. I never knew I could be so aware of my own skin. The girl gestured that she wanted to touch my red hair.

"What do I do?" I whispered to Dre.

"I think you bend down." He grinned.

As she touched my head, the villagers murmured. Soon another kid approached, and then more. With so many hands in my hair, I felt like a dog on a schoolyard. But the grown-ups were chuckling, and the children were happy.

They followed us everywhere we went. It was distracting, especially when we were putting together the bookshelves. Every time I dropped my screwdriver—which was often—someone ran to help me. And every time, they stroked my hair or my arm as they left. Mr. Gallagher asked if I'd like to work by myself for a while.

"I need someone to paint ABCs," he offered.

I nodded and followed him around to the back of the school, where a new blackboard leaned against the stilts. Although this was on the edge of the jungle, I could still see Dre, Noelle and the village kids not that far away. The barrier created by the bookshelves wasn't perfect, but it would keep people from wandering over as I worked.

"You'll have to use white oil paint on the board," Mr. G. said. "The Yaguas' natural stains won't stand out on the black."

He left, and I started tracing out the letters. After I finished a few, I stood back to look at them.

I heard someone approaching. When I turned, no one was there. I peered through the stilts for the others, but they were gone too. The light was fading, and I hadn't finished. I shook the paint can and pried off the lid.

A twig snapped behind me. I heard voices. I spun around, but I was definitely alone.

Still holding the lid, I turned back to my work. A ribbon of white streamed from my hand. I looked down. The plants all around me were spattered in un-rain-forest-friendly white paint. I heard a squeal from the jungle. Or maybe it came from me. Would the villagers be mad at me for getting paint all over the plants?

Maybe I could wipe them clean. I grabbed a rag and started rubbing. Paint smeared everywhere, all over my hands and all over the leaves. I tried to rinse it away with my drinking water, but the water only beaded off, and the leaves stayed white. I took a deep breath. My only other option was to rip out the paint-smeared plants. I yanked and tore until I had removed every spattered leaf. I shoved them all into some bushes and hoped no one would notice. Plants were always growing back around here, right?

There was a breathy noise behind me again. Like a whistle.

I tried not to think about El Tunchi.

I took one more glance to make sure the bushes hid everything. The leaves rustled, and a creature emerged. It was a frog as big as my hand, with glistening black eyes. Instead of hopping, it lurched. But freakier than that…it was covered in ghostly white paint!

My brain scrambled to find a way to get rid of this evidence. I had to get the paint off, but I didn't want to hurt the frog. I scooped it up, ripped out another leaf and swiped it over the frog's back.

"I'm so sorry, little guy," I whispered.

The leaf helped a bit. I rubbed harder. The frog went limp against my palm. I lifted the leaf and peered at him. He wasn't moving. I poked him with my finger. Nothing.

"Oh, please, don't be dead."

But I didn't have much hope. I knew that frogs breathe through their skin. And this one's skin was covered in paint.

I put him on the ground, hoping he would hop away. He just lay there. I nudged him toward the bush. If only he would take a tiny jump or two. Then at least he'd be hidden and no one would see what I'd done.

Well, almost no one. I heard the whistling again.

Fui fui fui fui fui.

It couldn't be. It had to be my imagination. But no. This whistle was clear. It was close. And it was definitely *fui fui fui.*

I shoved the frog into the bushes and ran.

Chapter Ten

Running between two stands of trees, I flew toward the circular hut in the middle of the village. But I couldn't ditch the *fui fui fui*. If anything, it was getting louder.

I pushed hard, deked to the right and tried to avoid something black and rubbery. I tripped and went crashing to the ground. As I skidded through the dirt,

I realized what I'd seen—a Jaguar Jungle Lodge boot.

Chest aching, I glanced back and found myself staring at a pair of camouflage pants. I shifted my gaze up to a Bob Marley T-shirt and a familiar face.

"You interrupted my El Tunchi story!" Dre complained.

He stopped recording.

"Listen." He made the noise again. *"Fui fui fui.* Not bad, eh?"

I willed myself to stop shaking. He'd been standing behind the trees recording the El Tunchi story the entire time I'd been panicking about the frog.

His face broke into a grin. "Actually, it's totally funny the way you flew in right at the freaky part. Quality YouTube material, dude!"

He extended his arm for a fist bump.

"I live to entertain your viewers," I said, holding out my own fist.

Dre helped me to my feet.

"I'm also supposed to tell you we're leaving soon," he said.

"Awesome! Just get me through that anaconda swamp before it gets too dark."

The shadows were already growing, and it was only four o'clock.

By six, we were back in the canteen. We found Maria and Oscar playing Snakes and Ladders with their mom and Mrs. G.

"How was your day?" Mrs. Gallagher asked.

"Totally different," Noelle said. "It was like today we were part of the village and yesterday was all a big act."

"It kinda was," Maria's mom said. "The guides bring tourists to see a native Yagua performance. And the villagers are happy they get customers for their crafts."

"But the tourists left," Noelle said. "We were the only ones there."

Maria grinned. "You *were* the tourists."

Noelle's hand went to the dyed seeds around her neck. "Oh, I get it."

"All right then, Isabelle." Mrs. G. turned to Maria's mom. "You promised you'd introduce me to those parrots."

At the mention of the bratty birds, Isabelle winked at us. She led Mrs. G. in the direction of the kitchen garden.

After they'd left, Maria whispered to Noelle, "So hey, how 'bout that sleepover? I could crash in your room for the next couple of nights."

Noelle grinned. "That would be awesome!"

"No, it would not," Oscar growled.

"Come on, Oscar," Noelle pleaded. "We haven't seen each other all day."

Oscar put his hands on his hips and glared at Maria. "Since those guys came, you just hang out with them all the time. Who am *I* supposed to play with?"

Maria pretended not to hear.

After dinner she took us to a closet next to the bathroom and pulled down a basket from the top shelf.

"We can hide your key in here," she said to Noelle. "That way we can both get into the room whenever we want. It's better than the plant pot Oscar and I use."

Dre snorted. "Or you could leave the door unlocked, like we do."

Oscar crossed his arms. "This is totally no fair."

"It's just for a couple of nights, Oscar," Maria said.

"But couldn't we *all* just sleep in the bunkroom?" he whined.

"Yeah, no." Noelle bit her lip and smiled. "I don't think Mrs. Gallagher would go for that!"

"Look, buddy." Maria took a deep breath. "Why don't we all go fishing tomorrow after supper?"

"Fine," Oscar agreed, but he didn't uncross his arms.

"We'll need life jackets for the fishing boat," Maria said. "We should grab some now and keep them in our rooms so the other guests don't get them first."

There were life jackets for Dre, Noelle and me, but Maria had to dig deeper in the closet to look for another two. When she stepped out, she had only one more—and a sheepish look for Oscar.

Without needing her to explain, he stomped off toward his room.

"Maybe you can borrow one from Armando!" Maria called.

"Should we go after him?" Noelle asked.

"Yeah." Maria rolled her eyes. "Mom gets mad at *me* if he wanders around in the dark."

Dre waved goodnight to the girls. He had put on his jaguar-spotted life jacket. And he was still wearing his jungle-issue rubber boots and rainbow-colored bandanna.

"You look like a total nutbar!" I snickered, punching his chest.

"I know," he said.

He gave me his wildest grin and forced me into a headlock. It felt great to have my buddy back.

For once, I fell asleep as soon as my head hit the pillow. But I didn't stay that way for long. A tapping on our door woke me up.

"Jeez," I muttered.

Had Dre really chosen tonight to lock himself out?

"Coming," I mumbled, struggling with my mosquito netting. I swung my legs over the side of the bed, turned on my flashlight and found myself staring at Dre. And he was staring right back.

"I thought that was you at the door," he hissed.

"Yeah. And I thought it was you."

He shook his head and padded across the room. I don't know why it didn't cross my mind that he would open the door. It makes sense. Someone knocks on the door, you answer it. Except when you're in the Amazon rainforest in the middle of the night and you have no idea who—or what—might be on the other side.

But Dre didn't know that I'd killed a frog and destroyed a good part of the jungle that day.

Chapter Eleven

"Dre, no!" I croaked.

He didn't hear me. Fortunately, neither did Noelle, who came into view as he pulled open the door. Her brown eyes sparkled.

"We're going on a night hike," she whispered.

Maria shoved Noelle forward and followed her into the room. "It's so awesome out there just before dawn. Super dark and creepy. And it's when *all* the really cool wildlife is prowling around." She paused to take a breath. "You comin'?"

"Heck yeah!" Dre said, already pulling his hoodie on over his pajamas.

I grabbed my old yellow one hanging at the end of my bed and realized I owed Mom big-time for buying me new pj's. Thanks to her, I wasn't sporting a giant Pikachu on my chest in front of two girls.

We crept down the walkway and onto the grass. There was no one around, but the night felt alive. A million creatures screeched and croaked. I still didn't have my phone, but Dre filmed everything, from the torches sputtering outside the canteen to the sliver of moonlight down by the quebrada.

"Are we going down there?" I asked Maria.

She shook her head. "Too dangerous."

"Gators?" Dre asked.

"Snakes?" Noelle gripped my arm.

"Pink dolphins," said Maria.

Noelle laughed.

"I am *not* kidding," said Maria. "Girls in the jungle stay away from the water at night. The river's full of pink dolphins. They're beautiful, but some people say one of them is an evil trickster. When it gets dark, he turns into a man and creeps into the villages. He searches for a woman to drag back to the water with him."

"Oh great." Noelle wasn't laughing anymore.

I tried to crack a joke. "Like there aren't enough real creepy things trolling that river. There have to be legends about possessed dolphins too!"

Noelle relaxed her grip but kept holding my arm. Maria walked ahead, and Dre followed her with his camera. For the first time, I was glad none of the other guys from school had come down here with us. I liked that Noelle thought *I* could protect her. I held my flashlight in my left hand and swept the beam from side to side as we walked.

"Whoa!" she said. "What was that?"

I directed the light to where Noelle was pointing. There, on a branch, was the frog I'd killed that day. It couldn't be, I knew. But still, it was the biggest frog I had ever seen, and its black eyes glistened as it stared directly at me. I gulped and kept moving. I didn't want to see if there were any white smears on its back.

This part of the jungle was swampier than the area we'd explored on the first day. I had no sense of how far we'd walked from the lodge or which way would take us back. I just hoped we weren't in giant anaconda territory.

"Shhh." Maria stopped. "This is the place I wanted to show you. It's totally sick!"

Dre swept his flashlight beam through the bushes, illuminating the trees and plants all around us. He paused on the water to our right. "What's that?"

I stared at the floating weeds and branches. Two yellow eyes stared back at me. In the dark water, I could see the long gray jaws and scaly tail of a predator lying in wait.

"I thought you said there were no gators," Dre said to Maria.

"There aren't," she responded. "That's a caiman."

"And that's different *how*?" he asked.

"I don't know," she said. "I think they're bigger."

I backed up a few steps. "Um, how 'bout we go back and ask Armando about that?"

Maria nodded. "But don't tell him we were out here, okay? I'm not allowed in the jungle at night."

"I wonder why," Noelle whispered to me.

On the way back to the lodge, we all walked faster. As we came out of the bushes, the night noises gave way to a clattering of dishes. I was enticed by the smell of something cooking. We approached the canteen, and I saw Mrs. G. sitting inside, her hands cupped around her morning coffee.

Dre looked at Maria.

"I'll catch you later," he said. "I hear a cup of cocoa calling my name."

I looked down at my yellow hoodie and green pajama pants. "I think I'll change first," I told the girls.

As I passed the canteen, I saw Dre through the screens. He walked past the hot-drinks table and sat down with Mrs. G., leaning in close as if he didn't want others to hear him. What the heck was going on with that guy? Normally, it wouldn't have bothered me that he'd been acting weird since we got here. But right now, when I'd just started thinking we were buddies again, I had to wonder what he was hiding from me.

Outside our room, I stopped to pull off my boots. As I straightened up, I noticed that our door was ajar. Someone had been in there, and this time no one was going to tell me it was an oversized bird!

I pushed the door open so hard that it crashed against the wall. *That* would surprise anyone still lurking inside. But the room was empty, and everything looked exactly as we had left it—everything except my bed. Someone had returned my phone and left it on my sleeping bag.

I picked it up to see if it was charged. When I pushed the Home button, the screen came to life with the last picture taken. It was a night shot. I hadn't taken any pictures at night. I squinted at the grainy photo, trying to make out what I was seeing.

It was the foot of a Jaguar Jungle Lodge bed. The netting was pulled back, and I could see the end of someone's sleeping bag. Coiled beside it on the mattress was a red and black snake. I could almost hear it hissing as it stretched toward the bag and the person sleeping inside it. On the right of the display was something fuzzy and yellow hanging from the mosquito frame. I looked down at my hoodie. I knew whose bed the snake had been in the night before.

Chapter Twelve

I raced back to the canteen, my mind exploding with questions. Who had done this? And why? I couldn't forget how everyone had laughed about the centipedes and the termites. Was everything just a big joke on Potato? Was that why Dre was acting so weird—he was constantly planning his next trick?

I threw open the door, and Dre's head whipped up. There was no one else around.

"Why would you do this?" I asked as I waved my phone at him.

"Do what?" he said. "I've been sitting right here since we got back."

"Well, *someone* brought my phone back. And *someone* took a freaky photo with it!" I lowered my voice as I continued, "When *someone* put a snake in my bed last night."

Dre's mouth fell open. "What are you talking about? Lemme see."

He made a grab for my phone.

I shoved it in his face. "And *you're* the only other person in our room."

Dre looked at the picture of the snake. His expression went from confusion to anger. "You think I did this?"

"After how much fun you had with the termite video?" I said. "And the centipedes? And *then* the whole thing

89

about it being Señor Diego? Why would you say that unless you were trying to hide something?"

"Don't be such a dolt. I was joking! We all were. What else were we going to do? Get totally freaked out?"

"Well, I'm totally freaked out now!" My voice wavered. I waited until I had it under control before I shouted, "This is a snake in my bed, Dre! This is a total jerk move! You're always trying to make me look like a loser in front of Noelle and Maria—and all of friggin' YouTube!"

"You're the one who's acting like a jerk, Tate!" Dre snapped. "Why would you think—"

"Why wouldn't I? You've had everyone laughing at me since we got here."

"We haven't been laughing at you," Dre protested. "I can't believe you would think…" He paused.

"Is that why you've been sneaking around at night?" I asked. "Looking for things to freak me out with?"

Dre pressed his fingers against his temples and closed his eyes. "Tate, that's not it. I swear."

He looked like he was trying to decide whether or not to tell me something. I couldn't imagine what possible excuse he'd try to sell.

When he opened his eyes, there was something in them I'd never seen before—at least, not from Dre. He looked unsure.

"It's just that...I'm not doing so great out here," he said.

He looked down and picked at one of his fingernails.

"What are you talking about?" I asked. "You're the fearless YouTuber."

"I'm not saying I'm scared of stuff! But...don't you kind of miss your mom and dad and everything?"

I thought about Mom and Dad, and about how much I'd wanted them when I was scared in the night. And then I thought about my brother, Noah, and his annoying mature act. I really didn't miss *that* at all!

"Sure," I said. "I guess, sorta."

Dre went back to picking his fingernail. I realized *sorta* wasn't the answer he was looking for.

"But I'm not doing great about other stuff," I said.

"What stuff?" Dre asked.

"Oh, you know, like anacondas and caimans…and dragging our butts through dark, muddy water full of monsters."

Dre snorted. I couldn't help the smile that pulled at my mouth.

"Okay, too much," I said. "But you get it."

"Oh, I get it." He sighed. "*I've* been totally lame. You've been canoeing through anaconda land and confronting your worst nightmares. I've been running to Mrs. G. every night."

"*That's* where you've been going?" I asked.

The noises in the room, the door *snick*ing closed—it had all been Dre.

He looked away. "I just...she gets it. She stayed back yesterday 'cause I needed her to send a message to Granny." He looked back at me. "I know. Pathetic, right?"

"Hey," I said. "If you want to challenge me for the title of Total Lame-o, you're going to have to get more pathetic than that. Watch the playback on your camera. You caught every major screwup I ever made."

"Hmm." Dre nodded. "I kinda did. But I didn't play those tricks. That wasn't me."

"I know," I said, looking at the picture on my phone again. "And it wasn't an evil toucan either."

Dre squirmed. "I hear ya. But Tate…"

He took a deep breath. "If it wasn't me—and it *obviously* wasn't Señor Diego—then who the heck brought a snake into our room last night?"

"I don't know," I said.

It couldn't hurt to tell him one more thing. I launched into the story about the paint and the frog and how I'd been sure I'd heard someone watching me even before he was recording his *fui fui fui*.

I expected him to laugh. It would have felt better if he had. But instead he looked at me seriously.

"You don't think it was El Tunchi?"

I didn't answer. Both of us knew there had to be another explanation. So we sat there in silence, hoping the other would come up with it.

The canteen door creaked open.

"Guys!" Armando said as he walked in with Mrs. Gallagher. "Why am I seeing such unhappy faces?"

We both shrugged.

Mrs. G. glanced from Dre to me. She raised her eyebrows. How did she always know?

"Well," she said, "we just came to tell you that Isabelle is taking Noelle and her kids swimming this afternoon. She wanted to invite you too."

I went ice cold. Swimming in the Amazon? Plunging into a watery realm of nightmares and monsters? Um, no, thank you!

As I faltered, Armando grinned and rubbed his hands together. "Or maybe we could use some guy time! How about a fishing trip?"

I nodded like a bobblehead doll. "Yeah, fishing sounds great!"

Relief flooded through my veins. Dodged *that* bullet.

But Dre cast a glance at me.

"Fishing? Like in a boat on the water?" he asked Armando.

"Of course!" Armando replied. "How else are you going to catch piranhas?"

I stared at Dre. Maybe I hadn't dodged a bullet after all. I had killed a frog and angered a vengeful jungle spirit. Now I was going out on piranha-infested water. If the jungle did want revenge, I couldn't imagine a better time for it to attack.

Chapter Thirteen

That morning, everyone from the lodge was going to the opening of the Yagua school. I wanted to be excited about the celebration, but I couldn't get my mind off piranha fishing. And the snake. Was it still in our room?

Five canoes were waiting to carry us to the village. Dre and I climbed into one with Armando. When we pulled away before the others, I grabbed my chance to talk to our guide in private.

"So what do I do if there was a snake in my bed?" I said to his back.

Armando's shoulders straightened. He rested his pole across the bow of the canoe and took a deep breath. When he turned to look at me, his eyes were round and wide.

"What kind of a snake?"

"Um…a red and black one."

"Was it red and black—*and yellow*?" he asked.

"I don't think so."

He let out his breath and grinned. "Then there is no problem! We have a saying: Red touches yellow, you're one dead fellow. Red touches black, you're all right, Jack!"

"Great!" I said, giving him a weak thumbs-up. "Now I feel *so* much better."

He turned to face forward. But there was no way I was going to bed that night knowing that the snake might be there. I was *not* Jack, and this was not all right!

At the Yagua village, we visited the school one last time. In the library, the children pulled down books and ran to show them to us. Noelle saw me looking at all the empty shelves.

"That's okay," she said. "There's just more for us to fill!"

We left the school, and Mr. G. was waiting on the steps. He gave a short speech to the crowd, and the children thanked each of us with a necklace made from dyed seeds.

"That's awesome!" Noelle beamed. "I think I lost my other one somewhere on the night hike."

We ate rice and meat out of banana-leaf parcels, and there were plantains grilled on the fire. The village erupted into a world of dance, music and color. I remembered our first day, the drums and red faces that had unsettled me. Now, as a Yagua boy rubbed red paint on my cheeks, I felt accepted.

When it was time to leave, we shook hands with Sebedo, and the children followed us back to the canoes. Each one stroked my arms or hair one last time. I grinned into Dre's camera. For once, I was glad he was recording. I never wanted to forget this day.

When we arrived back at the lodge, Armando asked us to give him five minutes and then he would meet us down at his boat. "I just need to get sticks for fishing."

I assumed that meant poles. But no. When Armando arrived, he was carrying three sticks like the ones we used for roasting hot dogs at camp. They each had a piece of twine and an old metal hook tied to the end. Seriously? This was high-tech piranha-fishing gear?

As we pulled away from the dock, one of the guides was washing in the quebrada. Farther out, another guide was swimming.

"Aren't they worried about piranhas?" I asked Armando.

"No piranhas near here," he replied.

I remembered Maria telling us, *No jaguars near here*. Yeah right. Instead there had been caimans and five-meter-long anacondas!

Armando steered the boat into the current. We rounded a bend, and the jungle closed in around us. The air was still and heavy, like it was in our kitchen when Dad had left a pot boiling too long.

We reached the place where the quebrada joined the Amazon, and Armando cut the motor. "This is where we will catch piranha."

"You said there were no piranhas near here."

"No." He pointed back to where the guides were swimming. "I said there were no piranhas near *there*."

"Oh." I swallowed. Had anyone told the piranhas about these No Man Eating Zones in the river?

"Anyway, you should be more afraid of the toothpick fish," Armando said.

"Toothpick fish?" Dre asked.

"It swims into your body and drinks your blood."

I cringed. "How does it get inside you?"

Armando pointed at the zipper on his shorts.

"What the…?" Dre almost shouted.

"Don't worry," Armando said, as if not worrying were really an option. "You just wear a tight bathing suit. And don't make pee."

Not noticing the looks of horror on our faces, Armando got busy chopping up a minnow with his machete.

He baited a hook with a chunk of fish and passed the stick to me.

"You must stand in the boat now."

What?!

Armando pulled himself up, and I tried to follow. My knees wobbled as Dre watched.

"Come on, buddy. Don't be a hesi-Tater."

I knew he was joking. "Better a hesi-Tater than get ampu-Tated," I tried. "Er, I mean, to have parts of you ampu-Tated. You know, eaten by piranhas."

Dre pressed his lips together, trying to keep from laughing.

"Oh, forget it!" I sighed.

Why did it feel like everything around here wanted to bite us, eat us or suck our blood? Well, *this* Potato was sick of waiting to become dinner. It was time to bite back.

"Come on!" I said, pushing myself up beside Armando. "I'm ready to catch some supper."

Beneath me the boat rocked, but not too much. I could do this!

Armando told me to put the tip of my stick in the water and thrash it around.

"So the piranhas will think something has fallen in," he said.

I splashed the water until Armando had a stick prepared for Dre. We plopped our hooks over the side of the boat, and within seconds I felt a tug on mine. I pulled back sharply to set the hook. Maybe too sharply. A flash of silver and red, and there was a piranha flying at my head! I ducked, and the fish fell into the boat.

"Good job!" Armando knelt down.

The fish flopped around and he grabbed for it, trying to stay away from its rows of sharp teeth. Dre churned up the water again.

I caught piranha after piranha. I was a piranha-fishing rock star! Of course, the one time I could have looked cool on YouTube, Dre wasn't recording.

"Maria will be grilling up a whole platter for us tonight!" Armando announced as he took another fish off my hook.

"Maria cooks the piranha?" Dre asked.

Armando snorted. "What? Did you think she would be scared?"

"Uh-uh." Dre shook his head. "Those fish are probably more scared of her."

Armando grinned at me. "Sounds like your friend is fishing for more than just piranha."

Dre looked like I felt when he caught me in my tighty-whities.

"Well, he's sure not having any luck with the fish," I said, hoping for Dre's sake to make Armando change the subject.

"Yes." Armando chuckled. "Maybe he needs better bait."

I had caught my fourth fish before Dre felt the first tug on his line. He wanted to call it a catch, but nothing had taken the bait. Instead, his hook had gone through the body of a small fish and somehow pinned it to a stick in the water. Dre pulled them in together. We decided to call the fish *Stickfish*. We didn't think Stickfish would be any good to eat, though, so Armando said we should use it as bait.

Stickfish helped Dre catch a catfish. And—after I caught my sixth piranha— the catfish helped Dre catch his first.

"At last!" Armando exclaimed. "Now we can go back!"

"Woo-hoo!" I hooted as I did a little dance, rocking the boat from side to side.

Armando, thrown off-balance, reached out to steady himself. For a moment, I saw terror in his eyes, and in that one split second, I knew I'd been right to be frightened all along.

Chapter Fourteen

When we got back to the lodge, a rowboat was tied to the dock, waiting for our later expedition with the girls. I grabbed the bucket of piranha and my fishy-smelling daypack. As always, Armando made sure we left his life jackets in the boat.

"I am going home early tonight, guys," he said, stowing them under the seats.

"I'll be here in the morning to take you into Iquitos."

The daylight was fading as he pulled away. Maria was on her way down to meet us.

"What did you catch?" she asked.

"Seven piranhas!" I held them up.

"I guess you gotta eat them before they eat you." She laughed. "But I've got to clean them first."

Dre took the bucket from me. "Need any help?"

"Awesome," she said. "Thanks."

I looked around. "Where's Noelle?"

"She's with Mr. and Mrs. G. and the manager," Maria said. "Noelle figured they needed a book-drive meeting. She's had them locked in the office for almost an hour!"

Dre laughed as he and Maria started toward the kitchen. I was still thinking about the snake in my bed.

"You guys go ahead," I said. "I've got something to do in the room."

Dre stopped. "Do you need a hand?"

"No," I said. "I got it."

I knew he wanted time with Maria before we left. That was the least I could offer after all the things I'd accused him of that morning. The grin that spread across his face told me I'd made the right call. If that was all it took to be forgiven, I was glad. But gutting fish? Really? Like *that* was super romantic!

Back outside our room, I paused. I wondered if the snake was coiled up in there somewhere. Just because it wasn't venomous didn't mean I wanted to be trapped with it. And, as well, there might be some new terror waiting for me. I only had to make it through this last night in the jungle. If El Tunchi would give me that, I might make it home alive.

I opened the door a crack. I could see gray shadows, but nothing seemed to be moving. I crept into the room. My rumpled sleeping bag was still on my mattress. So was my overflowing backpack. Dre's bed was a disaster. His clothes were all over, and a life jacket hung from the mosquito frame. I remembered dumping mine by the window. It wasn't there now.

I used my foot to shift my pack so that I could check underneath. The snake could be anywhere. I looked under both beds and poked through Dre's clothes. No snake, but no life jacket either. It had vanished—just like my boot and my phone.

Frustrated, I crossed my arms—the same way Oscar had in front of the supply closet. *Oscar.* He'd been furious when Maria told him there weren't enough life jackets for him to come with us. Now, he'd obviously stolen mine.

I ran out the door and along the walkway. The lanterns around the lodge were already glowing. Somehow they made everything else feel darker. I thumped down the steps by the bathroom and onto the grass. Oscar's room was in the corner of the L-shaped staff building.

I took a moment to calm down, and then I knocked. There was no noise. I knocked harder. No answer.

"Oscar!" I called.

There was still nothing.

I turned the handle. I knew I shouldn't barge in, but Oscar had it coming! I pushed against the door. It wouldn't open. Figures he'd know to protect his stuff. He and Maria hid their key in a plant pot so they could always lock the door behind them.

There were plants all over the patio. The key was probably hidden right here. Bending down by a flower,

I tipped back its pot. There was nothing underneath but dirt and bugs. I checked under another and another, but the key was not hidden on that patio. A single leafy fern grew in a pot on the grass. I peered underneath it too. Nothing. Still, ferns did a good job of hiding things under their leaves. I groped in the dirt beneath them until my fingers touched something cool and metallic—the key.

Checking to make sure no one was looking, I let myself into Oscar's room. He wasn't there, but there was a note on Maria's bed.

> *Too bad. So sad. I took*
> *the boat.*
> *You guyz don't get all*
> *the fun tonite.*
> *Oscar*

As I looked down at the paper, I saw the toe of a black boot sticking out from under the bed. I bent down to pull it out. It was a size 10. And there with it were

Noelle's necklace, Dre's purple bandanna and my life jacket. Oscar had been smart enough to hide it so we couldn't go fishing, but not smart enough to take it himself.

It was dark out there, and he was going out alone in the rowboat. If he fell into the water with no life jacket, he could drown. That was if something didn't eat him first!

Chapter Fifteen

I had to catch Oscar. I grabbed the life jacket and whipped around. A snake stared me in the face.

I stopped cold. My throat let out a strangled *ga-acck* as I fell back on the bed.

The snake's tongue vibrated. But it couldn't get at me. It was behind plastic, trapped in one of those bug-catching boxes kids use. Oscar had left it on top of his dresser.

"Red and black. Red and black. You're just great, Tate," I whispered as I ran out of the room.

I took a deep breath. The snake was not in my bed. It was safely locked away. And no one had angered El Tunchi. We had upset Oscar.

Whenever he had tried to hang out with us, Maria had said no. Noelle had treated him like he was her annoying little brother. And I had threatened to smush him! It must have looked like we were stealing his sister away when he wanted to be friends with us too. No wonder he was mad.

I ran down the path toward the flickering torches by the quebrada. A lantern glowed just beyond them. It illuminated Oscar's face as he tried to untie the rowboat from the dock.

"Oscar!" I called out.

He glanced up and worked faster. As I ran onto the wooden boards, Oscar got the rope untied and pushed off with his oar. I made a grab for the boat, but it drifted beyond my reach. Teetering above the muddy quebrada, I grasped a rail and tried not to fall in.

Beside me, the long mooring rope was unfurling into the creek. One end was tied to the dock post. The other was lost in the water.

"Oscar, come on," I said. "Come back. You don't even have a life jacket."

"No!" he snapped.

He struggled to get the wooden oars into position. They were way too big for an eight-year-old.

The rowboat was drifting toward the place where the water flowed quickly. I looked around. There had to be another boat somewhere. Or a life preserver. Or a rod to pull him back with. There was nothing. Only the life jacket in my hand.

Oscar shouted. He had dropped one of his oars in the water and was reaching for it.

"Oscar, no!" I called. "Sit down."

My voice was drowned out by the splash as he hit the water.

Seeing the ripples where he had disappeared, I knew I had to go into the quebrada. But my feet felt nailed to the boards of the dock. What was lurking below that surface?

There was no time to wait. Oscar was in that water, and every second counted. Keeping my eyes on the spot where I had seen him slip under, I thrust my arms into my life jacket and fastened the snaps. Oscar's hand reached up through the water. Then his head broke the surface. He gasped and started to dog-paddle.

But the current was working against him. I bent down and grabbed the mooring rope beside me. *I* was not going to be stuck out there with no way to get back! I started hauling the rope out of the water. Hand over hand over hand. It seemed endless.

"I'm coming, Oscar!" I shouted. "Keep swimming."

Slipping the end of the rope through my life jacket, I tied it off. I tried not to think of piranhas and toothpick fish as I held my breath. For once, I was grateful for my tighty-whities. I plunged off the dock and into the dark water.

Chapter Sixteen

"Help me, Tate!" Oscar sputtered.

I willed my arms and legs to move, but I was half paralyzed with fear. Even if El Tunchi wasn't out to get me, what was hunting in this warm water? Was I a tasty morsel swimming in an Amazonian stew?

Something brushed against my thigh. My heart stopped. Was this it then, the end? Did I stop to fight for my life, or could I outswim whatever it was and save Oscar?

My stroke faltered. I craned my head to see what had touched me. But it was too dark and the water was too brown. The current pulled me. Any farther, and we would be around the bend. How far was it to the Man-Eating Fish Zone?

I turned my face toward the lodge.

"Help!" I called, hoping someone might hear.

My strokes were weakening. My shoulders ached. I didn't know how much strength I had left. But I was closing the gap between Oscar and me. He reached toward me and went under again.

My arms whipped forward, and I felt my fingers touch him. He grabbed my hands, pulling at me until he had both of his arms wrapped around my neck. His terror made him strong. He was starting to pull me under. The water rose over my chin, my lips, my nose. I kicked out with all I had. Our heads bobbed above the surface.

"Oscar, you're drowning me!"

He didn't hear me. His eyes were wild with panic. I forced one of my arms between our bodies and twisted my shoulder. He struggled to tighten his hold. As he did, I turned him so I could hold him from behind. He clung to my arms wrapped around his chest. How would I get him back to the dock?

I heard a shriek behind me. Was something coming at us? My life jacket tightened around my chest. We jerked backward.

I turned and saw Noelle hauling on the rope. Dre was running toward the dock.

The tugs became stronger. I kicked my legs to assist. With every pull, Oscar and I got closer to safety.

But each moment I stayed in the water was unbearable. Panic rose in my throat as a post of the dock brushed against my back. I looked up.

Dre's face appeared at the top of the ladder. "You're okay, guys. We got you."

Lying on his belly, he reached down. He pried Oscar's death grip from my arms and helped him toward the ladder. I felt lighter in the water.

Exhausted, I hauled myself out of the quebrada. On the dock, I doubled over, gasping. Dre put his arm around my shoulders. I could barely breathe. Still, when I pulled myself up and let the air fill my lungs, it felt good. I was alive. *We* were alive.

Dre slapped my back.

"Well, buddy," he said, "I gotta say, life with you is *anything* but boring!"

Noelle looked at me. She was out of breath too, but the color was returning to her face. I tried to stop gasping long enough to smile. By this point everyone was running to the riverbank. Some carried towels or dry clothes.

Noelle put her hand on my arm—like she always did. But this time I wondered if she'd figured out that this Potato was kind of cool.

Mrs. G. bundled Oscar in a towel. Mr. G. looked over each of his arms and legs. Maria smothered him, wrapping her arms around her little brother as she rocked back and forth.

"You are such a doofus," she said through tears. "Such an annoying, friggin' little doofus."

Oscar peered through her arms at me.

"Thank you," he whispered before his mother hugged him too.

Making sure he could still hear me, I replied, "We're *all* friends, Oscar. We look out for each other."

Dre took his camera from Maria's shoulder. "I can't believe I missed all that."

He turned to me and said, "Get in there with Oscar. I need a pic of the dude who just saved a guy from the Amazon!"

For once, I would not look totally lame to his viewers—or to the kids back home.

Dre snapped a few shots and then said, "Well, Tate, we didn't let the Amazon take a bite out of our butts. I toughed it out for the whole week, and you've been swimming in piranha-infested water."

I glanced at the quebrada and the jungle all around us.

"Let's get supper." I grinned. "Right now, I'm all about taking a bite out of those piranhas!"

ACKNOWLEDGMENTS

Thanks, Mum and Dad, for having shared my dream of holding a novel with my name on it, and for the years of supporting, advising, listening and critiquing. All your hard work has finally paid off!

Thank you to Melanie Jeffs and Tanya Trafford, my two exceptional editors, and to the rest of the spectacular Orca pod.

A special shout-out to my kids, who each played an important role in the creation of this story: Ethan, who is anything but a potato; Natalie, an insightful–and exceptionally honest–first reader; and Dani, who knows more about creepy animals and stabby, bitey things than I can ever hope to learn!

I am grateful to Carey for teaching me so much about my characters; to Eric Walters for supporting me even after I chucked a peanut at him; and to Helaine Becker, Kristin Butcher, Sara Butcher, Suzanne Del Rizzo and her kiddos, and Jennifer Mook-Sang for their literary minds and sharp eyes.

The full extent of Marc LaBerge's contributions could never be put on this page. Thank you for sharing a life full of adventures, including piranha fishing and snorkeling with sharks. Thank you for being beside me, sometimes shoving me from behind, and for always encouraging me to just keep swimming.

Lisa Dalrymple is the author of the picture books *A Moose Goes A-Mummering* and *Skink on the Brink*, winner of the 2014 Crystal Kite Award. She has always been passionate about writing and traveling. While in Peru, Lisa hiked the Andes, swam in the Amazon River and even went piranha fishing. She lives in Fergus, Ontario, with her husband and their three children.

orca *currents*

For more information on all the books
in the Orca Currents series, please visit
www.orcabook.com.